QUINTELLIFY

Table of Contents

ABOUT THE SERIES

*"Small Business Growth Mindset"
is an empowering book series that
delves into the essential principles
and strategies for cultivating a
resilient and forward-thinking
approach to entrepreneurship.
Through a blend of insightful
anecdotes, practical advice, and
case studies, each book in the
series serves as a comprehensive
guide for small business owners
seeking sustainable growth in
a dynamic market. Readers will
discover invaluable insights on
fostering innovation, adapting to
market trends, and harnessing the
power of strategic partnerships,
all aimed at fostering a growth*

mindset essential for navigating the challenges of the business landscape. The series not only offers tactical solutions but also emphasizes the importance of cultivating a positive mindset. It explores how an entrepreneurial mindset can drive success by encouraging creativity, embracing change, and developing a resilience that transforms challenges into opportunities.

CHAPTER 1 - QUINTELLIFY

More than 500,000 businesses close each year! And another 560,000 start every year.

Quintellify: (verb) To enhance or multiply by five; the act of quintupling or making something fivefold.

I now have a new made up word that has never been used before. In the history of the world, it's not in any dictionary, and it's the title for this book.

Expanding your business by enlisting the support of four key individuals involves strategic collaboration and harnessing diverse expertise. The concept of having a team of four people come alongside you, two on either side as a business owner, to help five-fold your business encompasses the idea of assembling a well-rounded and complementary group. Here's a breakdown of the roles these individuals could play:

Marketing Maven:

Bringing in a skilled marketing professional is crucial for amplifying your business's reach and visibility. This person can develop and execute targeted marketing strategies, leverage digital platforms, and create compelling campaigns to attract a broader audience. Their expertise can help enhance your brand presence and draw in new customers, contributing significantly to the growth of your business.

Financial Wizard:

A financial expert is essential for sound fiscal management and strategic planning. This individual can analyze your financial data, identify cost-saving opportunities, and provide insights into budget allocation. With a keen eye on financial health, they can help streamline operations, maximize profitability, and guide the business toward sustainable growth. Their role is pivotal in ensuring that your business not only expands but does so with financial stability.

Operational Guru:

An operations specialist focuses on optimizing internal processes and workflows. They can identify efficiency gaps, implement streamlined procedures, and enhance overall productivity. With their expertise, you can scale your business without sacrificing quality or overburdening your team. Their role is instrumental in creating a strong foundation for growth, ensuring that as your business expands, its internal operations remain cohesive and effective.

Innovative Strategist:

An innovative strategist brings a forward-thinking perspective to the table. This individual can explore new markets, assess emerging trends, and guide your business in adapting to industry shifts. By staying ahead of the curve, they contribute to the agility and adaptability of your business. Their focus on innovation and strategic foresight helps position your business as a leader in the market, fostering long-term success and resilience.

The synergy created by these four key individuals, each excelling in their respective domains, can lead to a holistic and well-rounded approach to business growth. Collaboration among these experts enables you, as a business owner, to leverage their collective strengths, minimize blind spots, and navigate challenges with a comprehensive strategy. The result is a business poised not only for substantial growth but also for sustained success in the dynamic and competitive business landscape.

By the way, many of you reading this right now are trying to be all five of those people at the same time (I bet you are either smiling or rolling your eyes, saying, "How did Rick know?").

The right mindset for any business owner is growth. It also needs to be a mindset of hard work with a commitment to having joy and smiling often. Hard work does not mean it has to be labor intensive. You do need to be committed. You need to give it 99% almost all the time, but you also need to have a great attitude while doing it.

I'm Rick Saffeels, native to the beautiful city of Salem, Oregon. As the director of the Local Oregon Legacy Builders, I've learned some interesting things about running a small business. I still have a long way to go.

Close one eye: you wake up, pour yourself that first cup of (beverage of your choice mine is not coffee), and envision selling your business tomorrow. Sounds a bit nerve-wracking, right? But trust me, it's a game-changer. This mindset doesn't mean you're in a constant state of panic. Instead, it instills a sense of urgency and perpetual improvement. It's like you're prepping your business for its red-carpet debut every day.

Now, you might wonder, why this approach? Well, it keeps you on your toes. It encourages you to view your business through the critical eyes of a potential buyer. What would they find attractive? What areas need polishing? By adopting this mindset, you're not just managing; you're actively enhancing the value of your business. It's a proactive stance that transforms the way you operate on a daily basis.

Let me share a little surprise with you: the most successful businesses are those that are always ready to be sold. It's not about a constant state of exit, but rather a perpetual state of readiness. So, as you navigate the intricate dance of entrepreneurship, keep in mind the mantra: run your business like you're selling it tomorrow. Embrace the excitement of improvement, and watch your business thrive.

Now, imagine this: your alarm clock buzzes, and you wake up with a spark of anticipation. Today is not just another day; it's a chance to refine, innovate, and elevate your business game. As you sip your morning coffee, you don't just see tasks ahead; you see opportunities. Why? Because you're running your business like you're selling it tomorrow. It's not about frantic, last-minute preparations; it's about consistently refining your operations, ensuring that each day adds value to your business.

For almost a decade, disc golf was a huge part of my life. Yes, the plastic thing that people throw in the woods. After my first few amateur tournaments, I was ranked the number one amateur disc golfer in the state of Oregon. I moved up to professional rankings after my third tournament, and once I cashed after my second event, I never looked back. I would go on to win more than 50 tournaments in 4 years and 17 of those professionally ranked. I ran 66 tournaments throughout the state of Oregon, some of them for small organizations and events all the way up to some of the most desired tournaments in the Northwest, having professionals traveling from all over the country. I got endorsed by more than 10 different companies, being a brand ambassador for international companies and creating media for some of the world's biggest names in disc golf. I was coaching, teaching lessons, writing articles, and selling merch.

Needless to say, I thought I was all in.

But when I had everything I needed to be successful and move into a full-time career of touring and playing disc golf around the nation, and potentially the world, I gave that up to be a family man. I decided to stay local in my community, and to actually go completely cold turkey on disc golf. In 2018 I played my last professional event and didn't even play disc golf for an entire year.

December of 2019 is when I would start my first business called Saffeels Social Media as a consultant for a mortgage loan officer. Buddy Puckett gave me my first opportuniy to be a social media consultant and social media manager.

That was three months before the Pandemic.

Pretty crazy timing.

In the realm of disc golf, every shot is an opportunity for improvement. The same principle applies in the business world. By cultivating a mindset that treats each day as an opportunity to enhance your business's appeal, you create an atmosphere of perpetual growth. It's not just about attracting potential buyers; it's about attracting success. This approach transforms your business from a static entity into a dynamic force, always ready to adapt, evolve, and captivate.

As you navigate the challenges and triumphs of your business journey, keep the image of a potential buyer in mind. What would they find compelling? What aspects of your business would make them eager to invest? By answering these questions daily, you not only prepare for a hypothetical sale but also fortify your business against the unpredictable tides of the market. So, rise and shine, fellow entrepreneurs, and seize the day as an opportunity to run your business like you're selling it tomorrow – because the thrill of perpetual improvement is the heartbeat of entrepreneurial success.

CHAPTER 2 - "MARGIN"

Disc golf and business might seem worlds apart, but in both, the concept of margin reigns supreme. Back in my disc golf days, every shot required precision – a narrow margin could be the difference between triumph and defeat. The same principle applies to business. Whether it's making strategic decisions or navigating unforeseen challenges, finding that sweet spot in your margin is key.

Imagine each decision as a disc golf shot. You're standing at the tee, assessing the terrain, and determining the best angle to navigate the course. In business, it's about assessing risks, understanding your financial landscape, and making decisions that propel you towards success. Too wide a margin, and you might miss the mark; too narrow, and you could find yourself in the rough.

In the business world, your margin is your lifeline. It's not just about profit margins, although they're crucial. It's about maintaining a balance that ensures sustainability and growth.

BRAIN BREAK: PLEASE STOP READING AND GET A STICKY NOTE.

I was given a sticky note in college by my Resident Director, Justin Officer, and he told me to write down all the things I do in one day.

I couldn't believe it. I used up the entire thing and had no space, or margin, on the piece of paper at all. In fact, it was actually overflowing outside the edges of the sticky note. Justin Officer was a wise leader and still is today. He helped me to evaluate my day and try to create more margin. It's why I time block an hour with a 30 minute buffer in between meetings. It's why I say NO to more activities. Back then, I was the epitome of the basic Yes Man, trying to please everyone and do everything.

Maybe some of you might relate.
So when you are exploring the narrow fairways of decision-making, where finding the right margin isn't just a stroke of luck; it's a strategic play that sets the stage for victory.

In the world of disc golf, precision is paramount. As a former professional disc golfer, I learned that a match can be won or lost with a single throw. I would hit a 60 foot putt to push the lead to one stroke, to then hit a branch on the next drive and lose by that small of a margin. The same holds true in the intricate game of business. Each decision is about finding the right balance between distance and accuracy. This analogy translates seamlessly into entrepreneurship, where the margin becomes the delicate balance between risk and reward. Like a well-executed shot on the disc golf course, finding the sweet spot in your business decisions is essential for achieving success.

Profitability is often hailed as the champion in the business arena, but the concept of margin goes beyond mere financial metrics. It's about maintaining a delicate equilibrium that ensures not only financial health but also sustainability and growth. Your business isn't always about profit margins; it's about the broader perspective of maintaining a margin of safety, room for innovation, and flexibility to adapt to the dynamic landscape of entrepreneurship.

So how do we have margin in a crazy-busy, fast paced world? Lace up our metaphorical disc golf shoes and step onto the fairway of decision-making. Next, we'll explore how to assess the terrain, calculate the risks, and, most importantly, how to consistently find that sweet margin. Whether you're navigating a golf course or the intricate landscape of business decisions, understanding and mastering the concept of margin will undoubtedly lead you to the winner's circle. So, aim true, embrace the challenge, and let's explore the narrow fairways of profitability and success through networking.

CHAPTER 3 - "HOW TO PRIORITIZE YOUR NETWORKING"

"Goooooooooooood Morning!" was the phrase you could hear me yell each day, starting small and rising to a bellow with the word "morning". Then I would conduct with my hands the entire crowd to follow the same pattern of my voice, crescendoing into a mighty roar. Camp was the place it all started. My journey to saying hello to every person in the world and waving at anyone that ever walks or drives by me. It constantly makes my wife embarrassed, thus I do it all the more.

In the realm of education and camp ministry, I discovered the power of networks. It's not just about who you know; it's about who knows you. And the same holds true in business. Networking isn't a mere exchange of business cards or a collection of LinkedIn connections; it's about cultivating meaningful relationships that can propel your business forward.

Think of networking as a lesson plan. First, the icebreakers – those initial interactions that set the tone for meaningful connections. It's about finding common ground and establishing rapport. Then comes the core curriculum: maintaining those connections. Like any good teacher, you want your lessons to stick, and in this case, you want your presence to be memorable.

Consider networking as nurturing a garden – constant care and attention lead to a bountiful harvest. As I continued my enthusiastic morning ritual at camp and in the classroom, I couldn't help but draw parallels between my passion for greeting everyone and the art of networking. The relationships I forged during those summer days were more than just casual encounters; they were the seeds of connections that would grow and flourish over time.

To hone your networking skills, it's crucial to develop a mindset of genuine curiosity and active listening. Approach conversations with a sincere interest in learning about others, their experiences, and their aspirations. When you actively listen, you not only gain valuable insights but also create a foundation for meaningful connections. Ask open-ended questions that encourage others to share their stories, and be present in the moment, demonstrating that you value and appreciate the exchange.

In the world of networking, the quality of your connections often trumps quantity. Instead of focusing solely on expanding your network, prioritize building deep and authentic relationships. A few solid connections who truly understand your strengths, goals, and values can be more beneficial than a large network with superficial ties. Nurture these relationships by consistently checking in, offering support when needed, and celebrating each other's successes. This approach not only enhances the strength of your network but also contributes to a more fulfilling professional journey.

Adaptability is a key component of effective networking. The landscape of business and relationships evolves, and being flexible in your approach allows you to navigate different situations with ease. Embrace diverse networking platforms, from traditional events to online communities, and tailor your strategy based on the context. Whether you're attending a conference, participating in a virtual forum, or engaging in casual conversations, adaptability ensures that you can connect with people from various backgrounds and industries.

Lastly, generosity is a powerful catalyst for building lasting connections. Offer your expertise, support, and resources to others without expecting an immediate return. A generous mindset not only fosters goodwill but also establishes you as a valuable and reliable member of your professional community. When you contribute to the success of others, you contribute to the overall strength of your network, creating a dynamic ecosystem where collaboration and mutual support thrive. In the art of networking, the more you give, the more you're likely to receive, creating a positive cycle that elevates everyone involved.

CHAPTER 4 -

"PONDER PUDDLE
- SYMPOSIUM"

I magine the Ponder Puddle as a tranquil oasis where your musings are gently stirred into a symposium of creativity. As a camp director, I often found that some of the most profound breakthroughs occurred during quiet moments of contemplation. Other times it was when I was playing a game with hundreds of campers, or brainstorming with opposite minded people. The same can be true for your business.

The Ponder Puddle is a space for reflection, an arena where you can let your thoughts flow freely. It's not just about problem-solving; it's about fostering an environment where ideas flourish. Picture it as a serene pond where the ripples of your contemplation create waves of innovation.

Now, as you stand by the metaphorical water's edge, imagine the ripple effect of your contemplations. Like a symposium of thinkers, your business challenges become discussion points, and ideas flow freely like a well-coordinated ensemble. Whether it's a marketing dilemma, a product innovation puzzle, or a strategic planning quandary, the Ponder Puddle Symposium encourages a diverse range of perspectives to converge, creating a tapestry of solutions.

In the realm of camp directing, I've witnessed the magic that happens when diverse minds gather around the metaphorical Ponder Puddle. Anecdotes around the campfire transition into problem-solving dialogues, and creative sparks illuminate the darkness. The symposium isn't just a place; it's a dynamic space where thoughts intertwine, and the ordinary transforms into the extraordinary. A collaborative effort where your business challenges find innovative solutions in the synergy of shared creativity.

As you try to navigate a Ponder Puddle Symposium within your team, remember that the journey is as important as the destination. It's not just about finding answers; it's about reveling in the process of discovery. So, let the ripples of your contemplation extend beyond the water's edge, and may the symposium at the Ponder Puddle be a testament to the limitless possibilities that unfold when creativity and collective wisdom converge. Embrace the whimsy, foster collaboration, and watch your business musings transform into actionable insights that lead to success.

CHAPTER 5 -"HOW TO DUPLICATE AND DELEGATE"

I'm a proud father of four humans, and running a business and managing a family is the ultimate juggling act. But fear not, my fellow ringmasters; the art of duplicating yourself (not literally!) and mastering the skill of delegation is key for you to be successful.

As a family man, I've learned that the key to success is not doing it all yourself. It's about finding that sweet spot between leading the show and entrusting tasks to your well-coordinated team. This chapter is your guide to balancing responsibilities, ensuring your business thrives even when you're not personally juggling all the balls.

Let's start with the concept of duplication – creating systems and processes that allow your business to function smoothly without constant hands-on involvement. And of course, the art of delegation – understanding when and how to pass the torch.

Imagine your business as a vibrant circus, and you, the ringmaster, juggling multiple responsibilities. As we step into the circus ring of entrepreneurship, consider your team as a cast of characters, each with their unique talents. The lion tamers of your group might handle client interactions, while the acrobats could be executing intricate marketing maneuvers. Duplicating yourself doesn't mean cloning; it means empowering your team to become stars in their respective roles. Together, you'll craft a mesmerizing performance that leaves your audience – or in this case, your clientele – applauding for an encore.

Now, let's talk about the delicate art of delegation. As a former track coach for middle school students, I needed an anchor. The leader of the four part harmony that finished the race. The Idea Person many times starts the race, but it's the Anchor that gets the team across the finish line.

Delegating is like passing the baton smoothly from one athlete to another, ensuring that each pass contributes to the overall success of the race. Delegating tasks within a team is akin to orchestrating a relay race, where the smooth and efficient passing of the baton becomes crucial for the team's success. In this analogy, each team member represents a unique part of the team, bringing their skills and strengths to the race. Delegating involves recognizing the strengths of each individual and strategically assigning tasks that align with their expertise, just as a coach would assign specific legs of the relay based on each runner's speed and capabilities.

Much like a relay race, successful delegation requires clear communication and synchronization. The baton represents the responsibility being transferred, and effective communication ensures that everyone is on the same page regarding goals, expectations, and timelines. Just as relay runners practice and synchronize their movements for a seamless baton exchange, team members benefit from thorough briefings and updates to ensure the smooth transition of tasks. This communication fosters a sense of unity and shared purpose, essential for achieving the team's overall objectives.

Delegating isn't just about distributing tasks; it's about empowering team members to showcase their skills and contribute to the collective success of the project. Passing the baton smoothly signifies trust in each team member's abilities, promoting a collaborative environment where individuals feel valued and capable. This empowerment leads to increased motivation and a sense of ownership, as team members take pride in their designated roles, much like relay runners strive to excel in their assigned segments to propel the team forward.

Finally, effective delegation involves a strategic approach to balancing workloads and optimizing efficiency. Just as relay teams carefully plan the order of their runners to maximize speed, delegating requires thoughtful consideration of each team member's workload and strengths. Distributing tasks strategically ensures that each team member is working on assignments that play to their strengths, ultimately contributing to the overall efficiency and success of the team – a true representation of the seamless baton pass in a well-executed relay race.

CHAPTER 6 - "STUCK"

Ever find yourself stuck? It happens to the best of us. Whether it's a challenging disc golf shot or a business obstacle, getting stuck can be a frustrating experience. Think of this chapter as your guide through the rough patches. We'll share a few laughs, maybe a few groans, and, most importantly, some valuable insights to help you overcome those moments when it feels like your wheels are spinning.

Picture yourself on a misty morning at a golf course, the air filled with a sense of anticipation. Now, imagine standing at a challenging tee, the fairway ahead obscured by uncertainty. Where obstacles can feel as dense as the morning fog on that course. There's a poignant beauty in those moments of uncertainty, a beauty that lies in the potential for growth, transformation, and the triumph that emerges from overcoming challenges.

Emotions may range from frustration to the quiet determination that arises when faced with adversity. Raw authenticity of the entrepreneurial experience are the highs of achievement and the lows of navigating through seemingly insurmountable obstacles. Just as the golfer finds a way out of the mist to unveil the path ahead, being stuck can help you in discovering your own route through challenges in the business landscape.

When you find yourself feeling stuck, the first step towards overcoming the inertia is self-reflection. For me, its journaling every morning. At my breakfast table, by a lake, near a river, or in the middle of a forest. Nature has always brought me back to reality and the gravity of our existence on earth. "This world is not my home, I'm just a passin' though..." echoes in my mind whenever I need to take a mindful minute.

Some ways to help you get unstuck is to take a moment to identify the specific aspects of your situation that are causing the feeling of stagnation. Break down the challenges into smaller, manageable parts, and assess your emotions, thoughts, and any potential barriers. This introspection allows you to gain clarity on the root causes of being stuck, helping you formulate a plan to address each component systematically.

Once you've identified the areas that need attention, consider seeking inspiration and new perspectives. Engage in activities that stimulate creativity and encourage fresh ideas. This could involve reading books, attending workshops, or having conversations with people from diverse backgrounds. Exposure to different viewpoints and experiences can help break the mental deadlock and inspire innovative solutions. Additionally, take breaks from your routine to allow your mind to recharge. Physical activities, meditation, or simply spending time in nature can provide the mental space needed for creative breakthroughs.

Another way to help feel unstuck is to take decisive action. Often, the feeling of being stuck is a result of indecision or a fear of making the wrong move. Break the cycle of inaction by setting achievable goals and taking small, manageable steps towards them. Action breeds momentum, and even incremental progress can lead to a shift in mindset. Embrace the process of learning and adapting as you move forward, and remember that it's okay to course-correct along the way. By breaking down the barriers, seeking inspiration, and taking intentional steps, you can effectively navigate through moments of feeling stuck and regain the momentum needed to move forward.

CHAPTER 7 - "BECOMING A GIANT"

When it's all about growth – not in physical stature, of course, but in the world of business. Picture this: you, standing tall like a giant in your industry. Not in size, but in impact. It's not about being the biggest player in the field; it's about making a significant mark. Giants stand out, and in the business world, standing out is essential for success.

As the director of Local Oregon Legacy Builders, I've experienced firsthand the transformative power of community leadership. Becoming a giant means immersing yourself in the heartbeat of the town, understanding its rhythms, and contributing in ways that elevate the entire community. This idea is a tribute to the profound influence local leaders can wield like the positive imprint left on the community canvas.

BRAIN BREAK: WRITE DOWN THE BEST LEADER IN YOUR COMMUNITY AND WHAT MAKES THEM SO UNIQUE.

Think of your role as a local legacy leader as that of a gardener cultivating a thriving ecosystem. It's about planting seeds of positive change, nurturing the growth of local businesses, and creating an environment where everyone flourishes. Becoming a giant isn't necessarily just about standing tall; it's about empowering others to rise alongside you, creating a collective force that shapes the narrative of the local community.

Envisioning your business as more than just a participant in the local scene involves embracing a broader perspective that goes beyond the transactional aspects. Instead, see your business as a beacon of positive influence within the community. Consider how your products or services can make a meaningful impact on people's lives and contribute to the well-being of the community at large. By adopting this mindset, you position your business as a force for positive change, fostering a deeper connection with customers and community members.

To become a beacon of positive influence, prioritize social responsibility and community engagement. Actively seek ways to contribute to local causes, support community events, and collaborate with other businesses to create a more vibrant and interconnected local ecosystem. This involvement not only strengthens your business's ties with the community but also establishes a positive reputation. Customers increasingly value businesses that demonstrate a commitment to social and environmental responsibility, and by positioning your business as a positive force, you can attract a loyal customer base that aligns with your values.

Furthermore, envisioning your business as a beacon of positive influence can inspire a culture of purpose and pride among your team. Employees are more likely to be motivated and engaged when they see their work contributing to a greater good. Encourage a sense of shared responsibility and encourage your team to participate in community initiatives. By fostering a workplace culture that values community impact, you not only attract top talent but also create a positive ripple effect that extends beyond the walls of your business, leaving a lasting and beneficial imprint on the local scene.

My call to action is for leaders who aspire to become giants would not do it for the sake of personal glory but as architects of enduring legacies in their communities.

CHAPTER 8 -
"BLUEFISHING: THE ART OF MAKING THINGS HAPPEN"

Making waves and creating opportunities – "Bluefishing: The art of Making things happen" written by Steve Sims. Now, you might be wondering, what on earth is bluefishing? It's not about catching fish; it's about catching opportunities, creating ripples of impact, and making things happen. In this chapter, I'll guide you through the art of bluefishing, drawing inspiration from my experiences and offering insights into proactive strategies to shape your business destiny.

Imagine the vast ocean of possibilities before you. Bluefishing is about navigating those waters with purpose, seizing opportunities, and leaving a trail of positive impact. From strategic partnerships to innovative campaigns, we'll explore the techniques to make waves in your industry.

Bluefishing is not just about waiting for opportunities to swim by; it's about casting your net strategically, creating ripples of impact, and making things happen. The exhilarating feeling of being tossed by waves of uncertainty, steering your business towards success with purposeful intention.

As the owner of Saffeels Social Media, I've often found that waiting for opportunities to knock is like waiting for a bluefish to jump into your boat. It rarely happens. Bluefishing is about taking the initiative, creating a splash, and making your own luck in the vast sea of possibilities.

This chapter is a call to action, urging you to become the captain of your business voyage, steering with a clear vision and seizing opportunities with calculated precision.
It's not just about being proactive; it's about understanding the currents of the market, predicting the ebbs and flows, and strategically positioning yourself to catch the big fish. Bluefishing requires a combination of skills – from networking to strategic planning – all woven together to create a tapestry of success. Every action, every cast, has the potential to make waves and create a sea change in your business.

In the realm of getting things done, the concept of bluefishing encapsulates a proactive and strategic approach that goes beyond mere productivity. Bluefishing involves not only understanding the currents of the market but also predicting its ebbs and flows. It's about anticipating trends, identifying opportunities, and strategically positioning yourself to catch the big fish – those significant opportunities that can propel your business to new heights. This requires a keen awareness of the business landscape, a willingness to adapt, and the ability to navigate uncertainties with finesse.

To master the art of bluefishing, a diverse skill set is essential. Networking becomes a crucial tool for building connections, gaining insights, and staying ahead of market trends. A well-crafted strategic plan acts as the guiding compass, providing direction and purpose to your actions. These skills, combined with adaptability and resilience, form a powerful arsenal for anyone seeking to make waves in their industry. Every action, every cast into the business waters, has the potential to create a sea change, and by consistently honing these skills, you can position yourself not just as a participant but as a dynamic force shaping the future of your business landscape.

In the pursuit of getting things done, it's vital to embrace a mindset of continuous improvement. Bluefishing is not a one-time event; it's an ongoing process of refinement and optimization. Regularly reassess your strategies, learn from both successes and setbacks, and stay attuned to emerging trends. By evolving alongside the ever-changing currents of the market, you not only remain relevant but also position yourself as a leader who is adept at navigating the complexities of the business sea. Success in bluefishing is not just about catching one big fish; it's about building a sustainable and thriving ecosystem for long-term success.

Remember that you're not merely an observer; you're a masterful blue fisherman or woman, navigating the tides with purpose and intent.

CHAPTER 9 - "EXIT STAGE LEFT - HOW TO SELL YOUR BUSINESS"

Venturing into the delicate process of saying goodbye to your business – "Exit stage Left: How to sell your business."

As a former camp director and teacher, I know a few things about orchestrating graceful exits and how not to leave. Selling your business doesn't have to be a daunting finale; it can be a well-choreographed performance that leaves a lasting legacy. In this chapter, we'll explore the steps to exit stage left with finesse and strategic elegance.

Think of your business as a well-rehearsed play. The sale is your grand finale, but the lead-up is just as crucial. We'll delve into the prelude – preparing your business for the market, showcasing its strengths, and creating a narrative that captivates potential buyers. From there, we'll navigate the negotiations, ensuring a harmonious transition that benefits both parties.It's not just about selling a business; it's about creating a memorable performance that resonates in the business world.

Selling a business involves a strategic and meticulous process.

Here's a comprehensive 20-step guide on how to sell your business as an exit strategy:

Business Valuation: Determine the fair market value of your business. Consider financial performance, assets, market trends, and industry benchmarks.

Financial Records: Ensure all financial records are accurate, up-to-date, and well-documented. This includes financial statements, tax returns, and audit reports.

Clean Up Finances: Address any outstanding financial issues, clean up balance sheets, and resolve outstanding liabilities to present a clean financial picture.

Legal Compliance: Ensure your business is in compliance with all legal requirements. Resolve any outstanding legal issues and ensure contracts and agreements are up-to-date.

Customer and Vendor Contracts: Review and organize customer and vendor contracts. Ensure they are transferable and that there are no issues that could deter a potential buyer.

IP and Trademarks: Document and protect intellectual property. Ensure trademarks, patents, and copyrights are registered and transferable.

Operational Documentation: Create comprehensive documentation outlining your business operations, processes, and standard operating procedures.

Employee Contracts and Agreements: Review employment contracts and agreements. Address key employee issues and ensure smooth transition plans are in place.

Business Plan: Update your business plan to highlight the business's potential for growth and profitability. Include a detailed exit strategy.

Marketing Collateral: Prepare a professional and compelling sales memorandum. Highlight key strengths, achievements, and growth potential.

Confidentiality Agreements: Implement confidentiality agreements to protect sensitive business information during the sales process.

Engage Professionals: Hire professionals such as business brokers, financial advisors, and legal experts experienced in business sales to guide you through the process.

Create a Data Room: Organize a secure data room containing all relevant documents for potential buyers to review. Ensure easy and controlled access.

Marketing Strategy: Develop a targeted marketing strategy to reach potential buyers. Utilize online platforms, industry publications, and networking.

Screen Potential Buyers: Screen potential buyers to ensure they are financially qualified and genuinely interested in purchasing your business.

Negotiation: Engage in negotiations with potential buyers. Be prepared to discuss terms, price, and conditions of the sale.

Due Diligence: Allow potential buyers to conduct due diligence. Provide access to financial, operational, and legal documents for a thorough review.

Finalize Terms: Finalize the terms of the sale, including the purchase price, payment structure, and any contingencies.

Legal Documentation: Work with legal professionals to draft and review the sales agreement, ensuring all terms and conditions are accurately represented.

Transition Plan: Develop a detailed transition plan to ensure a smooth handover. Include employee communication, customer notifications, and ongoing support for the buyer.

Remember, the process may vary depending on the nature and size of your business, so it's crucial to adapt these steps to your specific situation and seek professional guidance throughout the process.

CHAPTER 10 - "IT'S TOTALLY WORTH IT"

We've reached the final chapter of our adventure together – "It's Totally Worth it."

One summer I was the day camp director telling all the stories, leading the large group times, the skits and songs. The phrase I kept saying each week was, "Is it worth it? IT'S TOTALLY WORTH IT!"
The video editor from that summer actually went back through and compiled a section of the end of the summer video with me saying it some 20 plus times, wearing different clothes and with different voice inflections.

As we reflect on the rollercoaster of entrepreneurship, family life, and those precious moments, I want you to join me in a heartfelt exploration of why the challenges and joys of running a small business are indeed totally worth it.

Let me take you back to the beginning of this book journey. We started with the notion of running your business like you're selling it tomorrow. The underlying message was about perpetual improvement, embracing challenges, and approaching each day as an opportunity to enhance your business's value. Now, as we conclude, let's circle back to that concept.

Running a business is no easy feat. It's filled with uncertainties, long hours, and the constant need to adapt. Yet, here's the beautiful paradox – it's precisely these challenges that make the journey worthwhile. The late nights spent refining strategies, the moments of doubt transformed into triumphant successes, and the growth you experience along the way – these are the threads that weave the tapestry of entrepreneurship.

As a former professional disc golfer, I know the sweet taste of victory after overcoming hurdles on the course. Similarly, in business, every obstacle conquered, every goal achieved, adds to the sense of accomplishment. It's about the thrill of the journey, the lessons learned, and the resilience developed.

Now, let's talk about the family aspect. Four kids and a precious wife – they're not just bystanders in this journey; they're integral parts of the story. Family life and entrepreneurship are intertwined in a dance of balancing acts. The late nights might mean missing bedtime stories, but the shared victories become family triumphs. It's about creating a legacy that extends beyond the business realm.

Throughout this short book, we've explored concepts like margin, networking, pondering in the symposium of creativity, duplicating and delegating, navigating through being stuck, growing into a giant, and the art of bluefishing. Each chapter provided tools, insights, and a sprinkle of humor to help you navigate the labyrinth of entrepreneurship.

As you reflect on your own entrepreneurial journey, remember that it's not just about the destination – it's about the totality of the experience. The struggles, the victories, the relationships built, and the impact made collectively form a mosaic that defines your unique story.

So, here's to you, the daring entrepreneur. Here's to the late nights and early mornings, the calculated risks and unexpected triumphs, and most importantly, the indomitable spirit that propels you forward. It's a journey filled with twists and turns, but as we close this chapter, I want you to know – it's totally worth it.

Thank you for joining me on this adventure through the pages of this book. I know your business endeavors will be fruitful, your family life fulfilling, and each day brings you closer to the realization that, indeed, it's totally worth it. Onward on your journey, your victories, and the endless possibilities that lie ahead.

Be a giant, go bluefishing, become a legend for positivity, and lead with your legacy in mind to finish your race strong.

Because it's totally worth it.